MW01621176

WHY IS IT SO HARD TO KILL YOU?

SOMONDOCO POETS
HOPE MAXWELL SNYDER, SERIES EDITOR

Published by Somondoco Press
P. O. Box 3602
Shepherdstown, WV 25443

Copyright © 2016 by Barrett Warner
All rights reserved

Manufactured in the United States of America
Somondoco Press Paperback Original
First printing

Designer: Adam Robinson

Poems set in Adobe Garamond Pro; titles in Baskerville.

WHY IS IT SO HARD TO KILL YOU?

poems Barrett Warner

Somondoco Press
Shepherdstown, WV

For Julia

Poems

THE BUMPY LANE OF YOUR SPINE

I'M A RADIO ON TWO LEGS

SUN SPOTS ON THE RIALTO

THE BUMPY LANE OF YOUR SPINE

I Thought Pigeons Were Vegetarians

No machine can thresh grain like a bird,
especially the pigeon who downbeats
a throaty song and floats off
with nothing better to do than be faithful,
like its close cousin, the dove.

Monogamy isn't merciful.
Sunbeams stab through missing battens
as two newlyweds dodder to the peak
where an extended clan of bats
sleeps upside-down like grapes.

This pair takes its sweet time
harvesting a leg, a wing, a face,
resting between courses as if to relate
a story in a gambler's bluffing way—
shuffling, calling, raking the kitty.

Belief is a tricky beast
to keep alive on wheat and water.
Despite miles and days of crops,
and kept busy with the land's riches,
I never lose the taste for flesh.

Twins

The hand without feeling
resembles the hand that feels.

Both have sixty or so small bones
and five stocky fingers.

These hands have been friends
since either can remember.

Now, the good hand feels for both.
The bad hand waves, as if to agree with every word.

One side holds forth, the other hopes
that doors will open without knobs.

Falling on a muddy trail last week,
the bad hand broke the crash, cracking bones.

A valley cut across my palm
and two fingers refused to buddy-up.

In spite of its strange new shape,
it was entirely painless.

The good hand never stopped singing, nor once offered
to staunch the widening geranium of blood.

Poem with Only a Single Reference to a Shotgun

Someone's horn, burning rubber,
the thump and rip of a torn fender.
The animal—a buck with velvet
where the antlers should be,
crawls from the road to the pasture
on two legs broken from the accident.

I'm startled by his surrender,
turning his head to give me a better target.
The convulsions weaken;
his bleeding ear tells me I shot deep.
Now the work of tarping, and four-wheeling
the carcass into a wooded oblivion.

I toss a bucket of lime over the wound
to discourage thieves.

Peace Pipe

Staci Miller's boyfriend and I sit by rails
outside the plant's medley of soot and char,
our lungs in the usual panic.

The rush of October breezes rustle
through parts dying back, still clinging
to parts coming alive.

I squint to hide confession in my eyes:
what she said to me last night
about what I said to her the night before.

I don't remember how much I wanted
to breathe on her collar bone.

                                        Out here by the switch
her boyfriend and I twist brown paper into nails,
strike matches, breathe and cough
on the grocery bag cigarettes.

We must be men if we can do this so well.

Even Now, No One Is Talking About AIDS

Such a swift and silty river
after a long night of rains and split
trees and sparks prancing from wires.

My luminous retina burns to witness
as the dogs stare and shiver,
their heads riveted to the impossible—

a short log moving upstream against
the mad play of waters racing down
Devil's Hook. Rinsing its raisin eyes,

the beaver swims indifferent to our gawk.
There's work to be done, a storm-ravaged
warren of limbs to fasten shelter halves.

Logged

I cut things down.
When things are down I cut them up.
After I cut them up I consider my options.

You can stack what you cut,
or you can carry it with you. Sometimes
when things are down I don't cut them up.
I let them return to the forest.

Sometimes I don't cut things down.
It's happened three times already—
I drive into the woods and park
and sit and stare and think about Jeopardy.

Once after loading the truck I fainted,
knocked my head on metal parts.
This is hard work, cutting things down.
The man I work for wants to buy me a chipper,
and a machine that grinds stumps and roots.

I'm unsure. More options.
Too many gas lines to choke.
Lately, I've been thinking about the shape
of televisions and not the actual programs.

Heading North Are Two Highways

One is meant for anger.
It cleaves New Jersey into knobby halves.
The other is for crying.
At Scranton, it dog legs to the Poconos.

I draft behind a queue of trucks
with Carolina tags, and Illinois, and Maine.
We come from everywhere
and all of us are sobbing.

My mother calls. I blow my nose.
No, I say, I didn't get a haircut.
I didn't remember to shave my chin.
I am so blue, I forget to do anything.

Clearer than any sadness,
razors and rumble strips don't jive.
Outside Port Jervis, billboards
advertise truckstop masseurs by the minute.

I park between two idling rigs.
A man, beautiful once,
hip hikes into the large closet
as if he were still curious about love.

I can't take off my clothes fast enough.
He tries not to notice my bloody face.
How much does it hurt, he seems to crow.
It sounds like *Jesus. Jesus. Jesus.*

I Thought I'd Stop Having Sex Dreams of Kim after She Broke Her Neck

In dreams it goes like this:
outdoors, under willows, bodies quilted.
The more she takes, the more she has to hold.
The more I take, the more I let go.

I still had fantasies after she was married.
We were always naked in them
and there were lots of mountains—
snowy Vermont, the cloven Shenandoah.

Have some venison, she says, flirty, sarcastic.
Killed on the run, it's salty, gamey, like her
Kim's break is two knuckles down
from what they call a hangman's fracture.

After lunch, I wheel her outside to the herd.
A gray horse lips and tongues her ball cap
until it finds the peppermint someone put there.
This is the one who fell on me, she says.

Two-legged Animals Love for the Wrong Reasons

A few are lonely,
but most are just afraid of dying.

Talking bears are different.
Hungry, but shy,
we have to be curious to fuck.

Questioning, we defy our low centers.
Wouldn't anyone rather rake apart honeycombs?

After sex, once a year,
I sleep four months and dream
of Mary Oliver sniffing butterflies in the nude.

This is true romance: a blackberry feast,
and blindness to shame.

Bless her reverie. Once she watched me
clamber away in her vision
of making love to a talking bear.

No breeze,
the air heavy and still,
except two leaves on a birch sapling.

They twitched as if cracking up
at something the whole forest had missed.

The Kissing Class

Mrs. Harrison smells of chalk and dahlias,
tapping theories onto the gray slate.
Close your eyes, the teacher says,
feathering her fingers down my face.
Feel the trickle of my breath.

I close my mouth, ashamed
of what's hidden inside me.
Each day I fail the kissing class,
one more demerit
adding to the yellow bouquet.

Tanya

Florida. Know it well. Drank kerosene there in 1970. My father wanted to know why I'd drink kerosene. I was thirsty. Looked like water. *Did it smell like water?* No. *Was it a fountain? Were birds bathing in it?* It was a tank drum, I said. Skull marked with an "X" right above the word kerosene. He hauled me to the hospital to have my stomach pumped. The next day we visited the Execution Museum and saw an electric chair from the 1920's.

Last night, Tanya called from St. Augustine to say her husband was sleeping in the garage beside the Mercury. I listened and closed my eyes and sucked air through my teeth. I was so thirsty, lying next to my wife, who was plugged in to a book about Flanders, the cries of the wounded, mustard gas.

I thumbed an atlas, scanning varicose highways. What could forty years have done to Florida?

When my wife asked me for water, I reached for the bottle, drained half, and gave her the rest. I wanted to say, *because I'm a mean bastard.* But instead of asking why I had done that, she stared at the rain hammering our tin roof. She said, *Who's Tanya?*

Did I Tell You How Much I Liked the Maple Candy?

Maybe I was too unhinged
by the mare slipping
her eleventh foal
born the size of a cat
to imagine how
the air must have smelled
as the sugar bush sap boiled,
turning from the color of spit
to gray-green morning sky.
The mare's last foal
suffered kissing spine,
making him hurt everywhere
except in his quiet, lean gaze
as he galloped towards
a barbiturate finish.
Like him, the sweet taste
of maple on my lips makes me
reluctant to ever swallow.

Wind Music

Children's voices in the lower field,
and inside, small pictures clatter
face-down on tables, curtain pulls
rattle against blinds and walls and sills,
road traffic shakes the hiding forsythia
and the hair I woke up with is sailing
around my head like a gray spastic wreath.

Grown and gone, none live here anymore
except two horses, kin to the whole world,
and a few desperately chirping birds.
When who we love leaves, we burn the bodies—
the red pony, the retrievers and barn cats—
and store their cinders in sanded cherry boxes
stacked like condominiums under the piano.

My lover nests on the leather bench, staring
at middle C as pages of Schubert turn forward
and backward with competing earthy gusts.
There they are again, those laughing little ones,
and I rush, first to the window, then out
to the porch where two boys—but who are they?—
climb the fence and rush to the snapping river.

Black Dog

My friend Larry Poodle gets out of jail
so we throw a "Poodle Broke out of Jail Party."

Just another party at the dump—our duplex—
joined by the tank of oil that warms us in January.

A few kegs and blenders, and late into the evening
bodies fall asleep against anything that doesn't move.

Too shy to look at anyone, I hardly speak.
Someone's hand is grasping my foot the way twins are born.

All the nightmares lay beside all the dreams.

Larry shuffles from ash tray to ash tray, emptying smaller ones
into larger ones. He has a thing about fire. It's a new thing.
He never empties an ash tray directly into the trash can.

He is otherwise very smooth, with chuckling eyes,
and known for having the best Quaaludes in Tidewater.

About life, Larry and I have nothing to say.
It's the quiet hour that makes me so anxious.

I'M A RADIO ON TWO LEGS

Immortal One

Good morning, angel fish.
Why is it so hard to kill you?
The others were easy:
the green bird flew away
and returned to nest
in my Lab's soft jaw.
What of my Tabby mixes?
Crushed by tires,
decapitated by foxes.
Even the last of five dogs
stopped bringing back the ball.
And less than a mile from the door,
a hayfield where I bury horses.
But you? You refuse, in spite
of my forgetting your food
or new carbon for your bubbler.
Once I left you on the porch.
You lived for two months
eating uncautious flies
that sipped your tank water.
Come on little triangle,
is your song here not complete?
Why won't you die?

Thrasher

Reed is 32, but 85 in skateboard years.
Makes him older than my dad.

His stories make me think of fables.
Instead of ogres and orphans there are shovels and lawnmowers,
and everyday people just trying to sort it out.

Direct, curious, urgent; there's a tumble in his voice.

I close my eyes to hear every word.

I don't want to seem sleepy, so I pretend to look at the sky.
A church bell rings the hour.
Not sure if anyone else hears it clanging around the tree tops.

I love how Joan Miro spent 80 years trying to paint like a child.

The New Fantastic Empathy

The new look is in charge
of all the crying.
There is a sheriff of crying,
and a hundred deputies of crying.
There are nurses and cabs and cab drivers of crying.

Some laugh, the way you laugh
when you mean to cry.
The laughing and crying
are about the same.
The pain is the same.

I used to be the new look
(that was when the old look did all the crying).
Now I'm the old look
and the *avant-garde* handles grief.
Those kids are doing a fine job.

I'm neither happy, nor sad,
but the pain cuts me to pieces.

Falling Water with Forked Tongue, Somewhere, Utah

Boulders from the last ice age

divide the cascade's dive. I find a small space.

Crazy-made love means so much

with a Phoenician stranger, as if the less

I know the more I feel. Sadness

impenetrable, are we friends? In my pocket

a map of a halved Korea.

Cara caras nest a bonsai pinon pine

singing love-death, love and death.

My whirl is two bumps below your nape;

one I read, one I'm kissing.

Wing us here—beehive desert—where it hasn't

rain-dropped since Advent.

Maine Is Not the Place to Grow Bougainvillea

in spite of lakes and loons
and strawberries big as your skull.

A more thoughtful lover
would have dug out a birch canoe,
carved hearts in the varnished paddles.

For you, the water, the birds, for you.
Instead, I bring a tropical plant
to our lakeshore cabin

as if to say I'd rather be in New Orleans
with its crayfish and red beans
and salty Zydeco.

I imagine her sunning herself
on a chicory mat,
surrounded by Japanese poetry.

Bougainvillea
is almost
one-fourth of a haiku.

Mine is like an octopus,
thorny arms reaching over,
a yoga pose of pink and red.

That plant will die in a few
weeks, she says, *and then we'll all*
have to deal with your grieving.

When flowers die do you send people?
She backs down. The air and water
are too pleasant here, the midday sun

warming her bare cajun arches,
all too nice to argue the impossible.
Where do you want to put it?

Over here, I say, *by the banana tree.*

A Quote from Borges Might Be Cool

Two cars caravanning at night—
you followed my tail lights,

then I, yours. When you stopped
for corn chips and fifty dollars

of Texaco, I kept going.
Later, I pulled off the road

and you slowed,
averting your eyes from traffic,

then sped away as I waved.
I found a truckstop in Virginia,

and you, a diner in Tennessee,
but we ordered from the same menu,

ate the same biscuits and gravy and pie,
bought the same jukebox song

with shimmering coins, dancing
for each other, holding our own elbows.

Still trading headlights, laughing
and weary, we got lost in the Smokies.

How odd to find you five years
down the road hitchhiking in the Sonora

going east against my west, both our thumbs
shaking at blind drivers,

the yellow-painted lines cracked,
peeling up like molting sidewinders,

the bands on our fingers like we murdered
each other, and not some stranger.

Harvest Blaze

How much gasoline could I pour
on the smoking log before it flamed
the word *beautiful* on my arm?

Keep your plates of Jonathans and brie.
Give me peril, some extravagant risk
that mars the married soul—the memory

of a woman's gaskin belonging to anyone
other than my wife of 83 acres.
She knows me too well

to ask what I desire—would rather dress
her jealousies with small gartered furies.
The hearth smolders toward a midnight breakfast.

There are some sliced apples, she says,
reaching for my hand to feed or kiss.
I give her the one with a scar.

Ana's Older Brother Frank

Nestor and Rey Lopez del Rincon Gonzalez—
identical twins in the worst way.

To Nestor, I said my name was Jack.
To Rey, I said my name was Bobby.

They invited both of us to a party for their sister,
Ana, her *Quince Primaveras*, her Fifteen Springs.

My mother bought me a leisure suit
with wide mistletoe lapels.

Back then, she loved the Kennedys,
but now isn't so sure.

Jack can't make it, I said to Rey.
Bobby has band practice, I said to Nestor.

It was the first time I'd been invited
to a party that wasn't at someone's house.

Ana was a year older than Nestor and Rey.

Frank was two years older than Ana.
Always, always, somebody named Frank.

Pasta in the Nude

The pluck and snip of basil make me weep.
At least it isn't baby basil, but mature,
flowered, like it's been to high school.

Where is the pignoli stash?

We rifle through a pantry on knees,
heads to the floor boards. It feels cooler down there,
like I could cry without getting a fever.

Only walnuts. It's all we got.
Are you thinking what I'm thinking, Julia says.
I flip a lighter. You're thinking?

Walnut pesto chokes the blender.

We should have used the food processor.
We should have read the directions
on how to assemble the food processor.

I poke and stir the green walnut cement.
The blades unlock and whip against the glass.
The blender carafe shatters.

Does ruin appeal?

Smoke another. Reflect deeply. Isn't basil
a source of oxygen or ozone or something?
We gather shards and fit pieces back together,

adding meaningless layers of meaning,
my stoned Julia not too stoned
to add salt.

Insomnia

Stephie used to leave notes to Charley
beside her prosthetic breasts:
I've gone to bed, enjoy yourself.

Once she stenciled a bumble bee
near her dusky lip-colored nipple.
Honey, you're the best, she wrote.

He had Stephie cremated, but not
the yellow and black-striped bug—
a picture of himself.

Like Stephie, I left notes for Julia
about the snaggle end of my wrist,
its paw kicked off by a horse—

the new hand sewn on as if forever
trying to greet someone—its former
grasp lost inside her tremble.

I can't sleep. It's yours.

Claws

My stepchildren kill their suppers for a week:
oysters, clams, crabs—diving, digging—
eating with screwdrivers and hammers.
Returning with their Dad they bear a feast
of crustaceans packed in ice and seaweed.

I provide the *Racing Form* newsprint tablecloth,
glistening vodka, news that their Mom is away.
Her ex says he'll have just one (long drive and all),
pirates a huge tumbler from the galley.

A lot of work goes into crabbing.
Crabs are fast movers, and males are hard to sort.
Making drinks is hard work too. His hands
chisel a lime—green as my eyes—into sea stars.

Morse code for men who love the same woman
must go something like this: dashes and dots
spelling out that one could carve a sea anemone
out of another's face, or at least break a nose.

Strip everything to its humblest bone,
you still have two things, nerves and digestion.
There is even a shard of meat in a crab's elbow.
Eat the bodies first, he says. *Claw meat keeps for days.*

Exacta

Two gets you fifty the horse
will break its leg, the rider says,
locking my head between her elbows,
kissing and pushing against me.

This is what happens when jockeys
make love with gamblers—
the fearless knotted to the hopeless.

I don't bet favorites, preferring to back
overlooked also-rans "on the rise,"
or the bay filly she's named on
in a field of beaten claimers.

Time only matters when you're doing it,
the clocker says, eyeballing the fraction
of speed with the capacity to stay.

The real race is inside, along the hedge.
I wager hand over fist, whips popping,
jocks chirping, as I shout from the rail,
Come! Come on with the Seven!

We lose. We lose. We lose. I scowl
to keep the burned-out stump of a cigar
from falling off my shaking lip.

Thanks anyway for helping me find all the words
to endings never in doubt—*outrun, failed to menace*—
and for your shrugging break-up of a dismount,
your angry jog back to the jock's room.

I love your weighing out, swinging a bug's saddle.
The way you ditch your checkered silks as you reach
across my girth for the bottle of water.

Even at this late lost hour, it is sparkling.

Motion Detector

Staring at the motion detector
I try not to blink.
We play this game twenty times
a night, two bucks a match.
The motion detector is rich.
It has never lost, and winning,
throws a harsh light that blinds my skull.

The upside of so much failure:
I can stare a long time without thinking,
or making plans, or remembering.
But I wish we played for love,
or that losing would be winning,
and my fear of touching you
dissolved when I closed my eyes.

Luck has a way of drooling
like water from stone.
One night I bet a whole fifty,
like plugging another amp into me.
Of course, I blinked. *Goodnight my love,*
I said, into the white blinding star.

I Love a Crash

I come for the smash-up:
the spin, burst, and flame,
air so heavy with cooked crude
I smell it on my tongue,
guzzle the blackened calamity.

The bleacher crowd rains wings
and drumsticks on the battered verge.
Drivers pit themselves, needing fuel
and tread to bank the left-handed turn.

The clown drags a ladder
into the bedroom, waving
a yellow hazard flag. Very little
surprises a man with orange hair
and a tennis ball nose.

Velocity seduces,
and my love is the flaming collision.
Our smoke, ambrosia.

Reading Lips

Widening her elbows above her head
to imply *everlasting*, Cathy would sign
Heaven, rolling her hands in the air.
Eternities later I took up filtered smoke,
and George Dickel who stirred his own
infinite loops above the shellacked bar
on our whirling sour-mashed Sundays.

I told him about Cathy's mystery,
So silent, and so beautiful, I said.
George nodded into his Cascade Hollow
drink as if having his own reflection
on the rocks. *Deaf girls can't nag you*,
he piped; he ran people down like that
after last call, to let the whiskey settle.

I sat in my Pontiac, remembering Cathy,
while George stood outside peeing on a radial.
Cathy and I made love like dragonflies—
flying, swimming, alighting, restless.
Back then, in the country dark,
she shined a flashlight at my lips
to read my murmurs.

She Sits with Me on the Bus Every Day

Our dads drop us, we wait together. Then we sit on the bus.
We talk sometimes. We talk all the time. There are terrific silences.

Next year she is going to college. I am going back to high school.
And the year after that. And the next.

The bus isn't crowded. There are other places to sit.
Barbara always takes the window, and I take the seat beside her.

At my school, the boys' school, I get off, and the bus goes
to the girls' school a few miles away.

I've never been to it. Don't know where it is. But I like not knowing.
I like looking in every direction and wondering where she could be.

SUN SPOTS ON THE RIALTO

Janet Was Right: I Am a Bad Man

It wasn't something I could fix by swimming sideways.
That was how dolphins made love,
swimming sideways.

I perfected a kind of one-handed stroke,
the sidearm-butterfly-half wing crawl.
Beach police blew whistles at me all the time.

I wanted to be a dolphin and to make love
with Janet who sold small town bagels
and sang about Chevy roadsters and Paris,

going sideways across dirt roads,
full of chapter, and verse, and kissing,
and Solomon's modulated radio wave.

One day we found
a dead dolphin swollen in the surf.
Janet stared at the bruised tongue
hanging from the side of its jaw.

What can anyone say?—
mischievous breakers, fishing vessels, nets, and hooks?
It was dead. Janet, bless her,
never asked me why.

Sugar

My mother afternooned in bed.
Give me some sugar, she'd say.
I showed her my primer,
how well I could read.
That's good, she groaned.
Now bring me a Pepsi.

Our Frigidaire was crammed,
and cases lined the garage.
On rainy days we built Pepsi forts
and waged make-believe wars,
playing dead, clutching sodas.

At my graduation party
I didn't have to ask. I brought her
a bubbling Pepsi ocean swirling
around ice floes.

One brother didn't believe in God.
Bring me a Pepsi, she whined,
And drew a carbonated sign
of the cross on his fontanelle.

Another was a minister, and gay.
That's nice, now won't you bring me a Pepsi?
She blamed her rising blood pressure
on having birthed so many kids.

My sister was the one on the wild side.
Bring me a Pepsi.
I followed after her. No matter.
How about some sugar?

The First Baptist Factory Outlet

It doesn't cost so much
to believe in God, or pray to Jesus,
and the flock only sings the chorus parts of hymns.
I go inside, the preacher ranting,
Hell upside down don't make it Heaven.

A basket comes hand to hand.
I give it a dollar that's lived in a lot of pockets.
Wait a minute, son, the Deacon says,
You've got change coming. And in front
of everybody he gives me 25 cents.

God wants you to call him, he winks.
The next time I go to church
I put a quarter in the basket.
Wait a minute, son, the Deacon says.
This time he gives me a dime.

By the end of the month my faith
is reduced to a shiny copper penny
just big enough to press between
my worried fingers as the phone rings
and I know it's an old flame calling.

My Grandmother Doesn't Want Me to Leave

We eat wine Jell-O on her balcony,
made with Mateus instead of water.

Have another, she urges, like Manifest Destiny.

She made her Jell-O in copper molds,
this one, the shape of Texas.

Oh come on, she coaxes.
Just a piece of Amarillo? Houston?

Three Weeks After Easter My Vomit Turns Blue

The bones in a fish are all ribs.
I hide the meal—varnished with lemon
and sheaves of nostalgia—behind the box bush.

Here, under musk-scented leaves,
my family won't find my grandmother's
homicidal fried blowfish paprika.

My father in the broken surf—casting,
waiting, quietly dreaming—I should have spent
more time with him gutting skates with pliers.

I should have asked my grandmother
for the recipe before she got so old,
or if Cyanide would win the derby.

We used to call it *feeding the dogs*
when I first got sick and snuck outside,
our Labs racing after me to clean up the mess,

amid low-lying snowdrops that can only mean
resurrection, and in two months' time,
strawberries—fruit so fresh it spoils in an hour.

Wow

The *Yellow Pages* of everything
I might have been is slimmer over time.
At forty, I tear out all the *Surgeon* listings
when I notice the fluttering in my hand.
Already gone: careers in tumbling,
cliff-side geology (*that* was a mistake).
Would you let *me* cut your hair?

Twenty pages of *Beauty Salons* go into the fire.
I can neither buy, nor sell,
take apart, or put back together.
You wouldn't want me to turn a screw.
Adios *Plumbing, Electrical Wiring, Carpentry.*
The legendary lilac bush dies one winter
and doesn't return. I cross off *Landscaping.*

Fishing? The bass swim the other way.
Each morning I roll out of bed intending
to make an omelet but end up scrambling,
burning, scraping. Sorry, *Oregon Grille.*
I feel a sense of accomplishment
ripping out the future,
as if fewer possibilities make them easier to find.

I'm looking for a single listing:
Walking Around with an uncertain look on my face,
exclaiming, *Wow,* at frost on the turnips,
at the red smile of blood as I slice open a finger,
Wow, at seeing you leave, taking so little, as if
you'd be right back fifteen years ago, and *Wow*,
you didn't return once to see the lilac bloom.

Ricochet

The late afternoon's dark pond
reflects a red barn,
the sky's gentian violet.

My face in the water has a beard,
but my eyes are small green pastures,
indistinguishable from the water.

What surprises me is the hair,
longer than in 1974
when it brushed my shoulders.

I throw a stone at the reflection,
expecting the mirrored me
to catch it and throw it back.

Instead I hear the dog I gave away
and the dead mare at the gate
waiting for her oats.

Inside, the pre-dinner stupor
of wine and celery and potatoes
and something boiling on the stove.

Upstairs I shower and shave and spit,
turning to the sudden shatter of a broken window,
the rock just missing my ear.

Crow Funeral

Where do crows fly
when they aren't waiting
on the splintered fence line
for something to falter?

Nesting, does a crow
take care to lay every
twig and leaf just so,
each burnt coal or woven ash?

Maybe they prefer remnants of love—
a talon discarded from whistling embraces.
Second-hand romance is tasty
if you're a crow.

I'm not even sure they die.
Maybe all crows now are all the crows that ever were.

And then I find a dead one
planted face down on its black-feathered breast,
beak open as if gasping or choking
or trying to swim.

I'm surprised three days later
by two dozen birds lining a circle,
some shaking without making a sound,
others cawing about the departed.

A pretty one with a few white feathers
in her flipped-up tail preens.
A big one perches beside her,
turns his oversized beak
to exchange the sign of peace.

Sara, what are you doing here?

I Call My Dad on Mother's Day

Knew you wouldn't forget, he says,
without *hello*, as if I've interrupted him
at a very hectic moment of his retirement.

He gets *The Beachcomber News*, shares counters
at the Hard Toast Diner in Bethany with girls
who have flakes of salt on their faces.

I'm eating heirloom tomatoes, he says
through a mouthful. *You should visit
before I consume the whole legacy.*

Last year at Christmas, my sister
gave him a computer. Weeks later,
he emailed her back, *Happy Easter!*

For Valentine's, my brother sent an inkwell
and a hawk's quill. He used it upside down,
painting large black hearts with the feather.

One thing my father learned fast:
how to grow tomatoes
no matter how sad and sorry the season.

Shelling Pecans with Grannie Pat

Coyotes follow turkeys, that's what.
First you see turkeys, she cawed.
Then you see coyotes.
If there are a lot of turkeys,
next year, lots of coyotes.
Exactly how night follows day.

Grannie Pat's quilted face trembled
on the other side of her eyeglasses.
One son had joined the Navy
and the other had shot himself.
The name of that tree seemed to be
get far away from the San Saba River.

Doesn't day follow night?
Turkeys never follow coyotes, she insisted.
Night follows night, and dark, dark.
Once it is night, it's always night.
That's why ranchers build fires
and we always smell like something burning.

The Brig

I may come and go as I please if I wave my hand nicely.
Tuesdays and Fridays we get fish, eyes baked in the heads.

Lifers say you can't have a jail unless there is something
worth caging. This is how I know I matter.

Sundays we have a social if it isn't raining.
I wear a rat catcher blazer.

A few friends come over. Bruce shows me his jail—
lines hypothesized on clay in the shape of a cage.

Visiting my plain-spoken hutch, he wonders
what I could have done to earn a second pillow.

On clear days we can see a distant road, houses, a store,
smoke plumes, a cemetery where all the lieutenants are buried.

Hey, Look at Me

A black bruise stains the mind,
a squad of cardinals
curious about my crooked wrist.

I don't raise the window to shout
or wave them off. Smoldering darkness
weakens our reflection.

Such sweet aches, love's labors,
the harrowed acres inside me,
ditches dug with pick axe and spit.

I limp a chair into the room
and clamber on life's unfinished oak.
Changing the light bulb, right?

Those damned blue sparks wired
to a fault. Hey, look at me!

Even after I close the window,
nail it shut, draw the blinds,
the red birds will not stop pestering the glass.

Gira Mortal

Someone looking exactly like me
just turned the corner at West Broadway and Grand.

He was smiling as if he'd just had lunch
with a flamenco dancer who'd burst into flames.

He took long strides; no doubt she was tall—
taller than him—with hand-driven nails in her heels

and he was walking big as if pacing the memory
of her *gira mortal*, stinging herself with auto-percussion.

I followed him into a bar known for black wines
and cava and ordered a cortadito,

surprised that I could speak Castellano
like a matador on Benzedrine, all ego and hyper vowels.

Secretly, I'd always wanted to stroke a bull's hump,
so velvet, so nearly shapeless, yet meaningful.

Then I lost him. We'd been alone, now dozens
of crooked suede elbows at the bar made pistol fingers

and reduced their stories down to exchanges of vague,
but clever impressions, like shimmering oil stains.

At the hotel, I passed a large bowl of apples in the lobby,
and spidery clerks who looked like they only ate on Tuesday.

How was your walk? My cousin asked from the bed.
I gave her an apple. She bit a star into it. Then another.

Eulogy

My friend Keith Martin is dead. He died in early April.
It's kind of a busy month to die. The ground is softening—
rows raked and sown—jealous hues emerging like rye.

It's weird that he died the same month I was born.
Now the ghost will be forever Aries, the passionate one,
the one who gets things almost right, who gets in his own way.

A friend is a brick against the sweet hereafter. Lose a friend
and you lose a brick. Lose Keith and you lose a wall.
It's just a matter of time until the whole roof falls down.

Marsha, his wife, sat cold on offers coming quickly for his land.
I don't blame her holding out for more, but suffered lifetimes
are always cheap. I gave away anything I ever failed to sell.

No one wants to buy what you don't love.

Their house is a quarter mile away, through dense spite trees
planted by our neighbor so he wouldn't
have to look at Keith getting out of his car.

I can't imagine hating someone so much I'd plant trees.

One dog's not enough, and two dogs are too many.
That's how Keith would talk, like Ben Franklin.
He wanted me to feel better, but I never did.

Discount

We took backpacks to the A & P.
Alan showed me his loot: 20 pounds of steaks.

I got a can of tuna, I said, brandishing the fish.

Actually I stole two cans,
but I withheld this information.

I didn't want to tell him everything.

Nightcap

I beat the rat with a shovel,
but it still lives
to bite me every night,
a Capote rat with a complete
wardrobe of disguises:
a small sailor's cap for sea crossings,
a black beret for San Sebastian.
It follows me everywhere,
biting my hands and heels.

I say, *I'm sensitive.*
It says, *you take things too personally.*
I say, *focused.*
It says, *tunnel vision.*
Not *flexible*, but *spineless.*

You awake? it asks each night.
I'm sound asleep, I say,
and make snoring noises.
Small scabby stars of blood
constellate my chest.

I pull the lamp
chain, blow up darkness.
Ice cubes in whiskey,
a sweaty glass.
For you, the rat says.

Sometimes Temptation Falls from the Sky

If I see temptation coming
I'm quick to dodge left or right
to miss the small crater that forms
in the shape of someone lovely
and overwhelmed and alone.

I don't stop, not even to throw
coins into the gaping shadow
to wish for something different.
No, I keep moving, and maybe
I'll buy gladiolas and wine to go
with a half-shelled night of oysters.

I am leaning over the faucet
cutting stems on the bias.
Here is my wife, popping and
pouring the grape shots. Here we are,
sailcloth mitt and shucker, saying little
when she sees something
has bashed my head, leaving a lump.

Catching the Red-Eye

I'm the only passenger tonight
who wants to arrive at dawn,
drowsy and hungover,
three thousand miles from home.
Sixteen rows behind the cockpit—
why did they give me the middle seat?
I'm waiting for my tomato juice
and feeling blue for my luggage
in the almost-empty cargo bay,
a simple black dress of a bag
festooned in green ribbons.

At least I have Kooser, the pilot,
who's run out of ways to describe
altitude—our climb and soar—
and drones over the intercom
about North Dakota, the oil and people,
and veering now, he mentions
a place ten thousand feet below
where he went to elementary school.
If any children are waving back at us
from the last century, we can't see them
in the prairie dark, but just in case,
I lean to the window
and wobble my grieving hand.

Bath

Julia comes midday to the hospital
to smear lunch on my lip and to wash my hair and back.

Today's feast: bouillon broth and an egg.

She adds ice cubes so I don't burn my tongue.
Spoons it into me, dabs my chin.

I am ravenous.

I swallow three sips and go back to sleep.
When I wake she's gone, and my hair is beautiful.

Acknowledgments

Ancestors of these poems first walked in the following publications: *Cultural Weekly, Turnstile, JMWW, Black Bear Review, Fuck Art Let's Dance, Cloudbank, Freshwater, Everyday Genius, Espresso Ink, Ruby, The Tishman Review, Poetry Fix, Newtown Literary, Ilanot Review, Lines + Stars, Pembroke Magazine, Drafthorse Literary Journal, Common Ground Review, Natural Bridge, Two Bridges, Chiron Review, Steam Ticket, Little Patuxent Review, Princemere Poetry Journal, The Blue Max Review, Wayfarer, Shattered Wig, Backbone Mountain Review, Texas Poetry Calendar,* and *Consequence Magazine.*

"Sometimes Temptation Falls from the Sky" won the *Princemere* poetry prize and also appeared in *Seeking Its Own Level: An Anthology of Writings About Water*, edited by Denton Loving. "Tanya" also won the *Cloudbank* poetry prize. A few poems were reincarnated from limited edition chapbooks. One was called *My Friend Ken Harvey* (Publishing Genius, 2014). The other was called *'Til I'm Blue in the Face* (Tropos, 1994).

Kisses Palm and Blows It out of His Hand in All Directions

A weak person can't catch a train without a lot of people reaching their arms out the door and pulling him into the box. I'm grateful for early friends like Joanne Braxton, J. Wesley Clark, Jenny Keith, David Beaudouin, and Ed Bavis; and to more recent ones including Jessica Lynn Dotson, Courtney Sexton, and Suzette Bishop.

Big thanks go to everyone who has tried to teach me over the years—all of you should get raises—especially Tom Heacox, Joseph Hone, Diane Ackerman, Mark Wunderlich, Kim Addonizio, Robert Bausch, David Daniel, Major Jackson, Ed Ochester, and Ray Gonzalez.

I am indebted my publisher, Hope Maxwell Snyder, for hosting my work. Precise and driven, and compassionate, her energy made this collection possible. A few other editors have made a big impact on me or this manuscript: Adam Robinson, Edwina Trentham, Janice Lee, Anna Schachner, Janet Bowdan, Jennifer Barber, Kevin Higgins, Amanda McCormick, April Ossmann, Maura Anthony Snell, Russel Swensen, Wyn Cooper, and Stacia Fleegal. Mostly it was simply the confidence they gave me, or just the good work they do as literary citizens, but usually it was their sharp credible focus.

About Barrett Warner

Lives 12 miles from where he was born, like a box turtle.
Favors legumes over meat, and Bowie over Norman Mailer.

Often betrays a slight swivel when standing at ease.
Family members would rather not sit next to him on airplanes.

When the music stops he's the one still dancing.

Longs for a sense of community,
yet never knows what to say in groups of three or four.

He'd probably be the drummer, or the drummer's girlfriend.

Has an MFA from Bennington College,
but tends to avoid the room where it sleeps (beside the harpsichord).

Edits. Teaches. Panels. All that.

Reads with a pencil to underline the good parts.
Interested in presidential biographies, memoirs, and collected letters.

Cries during Boston Mutual Life Insurance commercials.

Enjoys a gentle vomit about nine o'clock each morning.
smelling faintly of raspberry and artisanal cheese.

Current affairs a plus.
Go ahead, ask him something about Venezuela.

Raises a few horses and other outdoor animals.

Wakes up at night in a cold sweat,
sure that he heard a funny sound in his dream.